In the Big Blue Sea

by Chyng Feng Sun
Photography by Norbert Wu

HOUGHTON MIFFLIN BOSTON • MORRIS PLAINS, NJ
California • Colorado • Georgia • Illinois • New Jersey • Texas

Acknowledgments
In the Big Blue Sea by Chyng Feng Sun. All fish photography by Norbert Wu.

Additional Photography
front cover, 1, 16, 17 Michael Justice/Mercury Pictures; **water background** image Copyright © 2000 PhotoDisc, Inc. **21** (inset) Norbert Wu; (background) Norbert Wu Productions **22** Norbert Wu Productions **23** (inset) Norbert Wu; (b) Bob Cranston/Norbert Wu Productions **24** (inset) Norbert Wu; (b) Norbert Wu Productions **25** (inset) Norbert Wu; (b) Norbert Wu Productions **26** Norbert Wu

Houghton Mifflin Edition, 2005

PRINTED IN CHINA

ISBN: 978-0-618-03638-7

ISBN: 0-618-03638-5

18 19-0940-10

I will swim in the big blue sea!
Come along and swim with me.

What color fish will you see?

What color fish would you like to be?

Dive and swim,
splish, *splash*, splish!
Would you be a green fish?

Dive and swim,
splish, splash, splish!
Would you be a red fish?

Dive and swim,
splish, splash, splish!
Would you be a yellow fish?

Dive and swim,
splish, splash, splish!
Would you be an orange fish?

What color fish will you see?

What color fish would you like to be?

Dive and swim,
splish, splash, splish!
Would you be a white fish?

Dive and swim,
splish, splash, splish!
Would you be a blue fish?

Dive and swim,
splish, *splash*, splish!
Would you be a purple fish?

Dive and swim,
splish, *splash*, splish!
Would you be a black fish?

What color fish did you see?

What color fish would you like to be?

We swam like fish in the big blue sea.

I'm so glad you swam with me!

NAME: **Queen Angelfish**
HABITAT: Caribbean

NAME: **Blue-spotted Grouper**
HABITAT: Indo-Pacific

NAME: **Three-spotted Angelfish**
HABITAT: Indo-Pacific

NAME: **Clown Fish**
HABITAT: Indo-Malaysian Archipelago to Japan

NAME: **Redback Butterfly Fish**
HABITAT: Red Sea

NAME: **Powder Blue Surgeonfish**
HABITAT: Indo-Pacific

NAME: **Blackcap Basslet**
HABITAT: Bahamas, northwestern and southern Caribbean

NAME: **Juvenile French Angelfish**
HABITAT: Caribbean

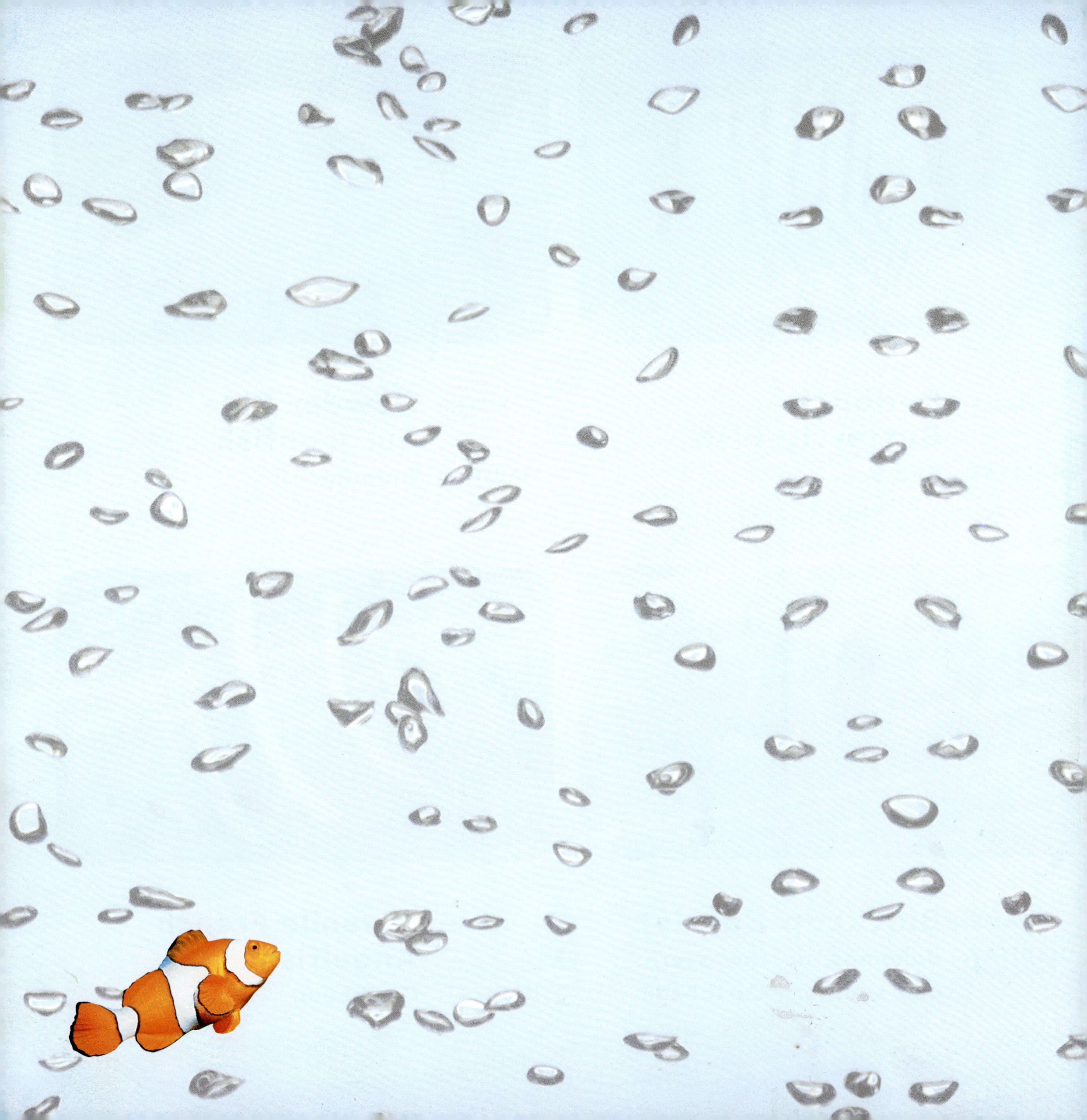

What Do You Do, Norbert Wu?

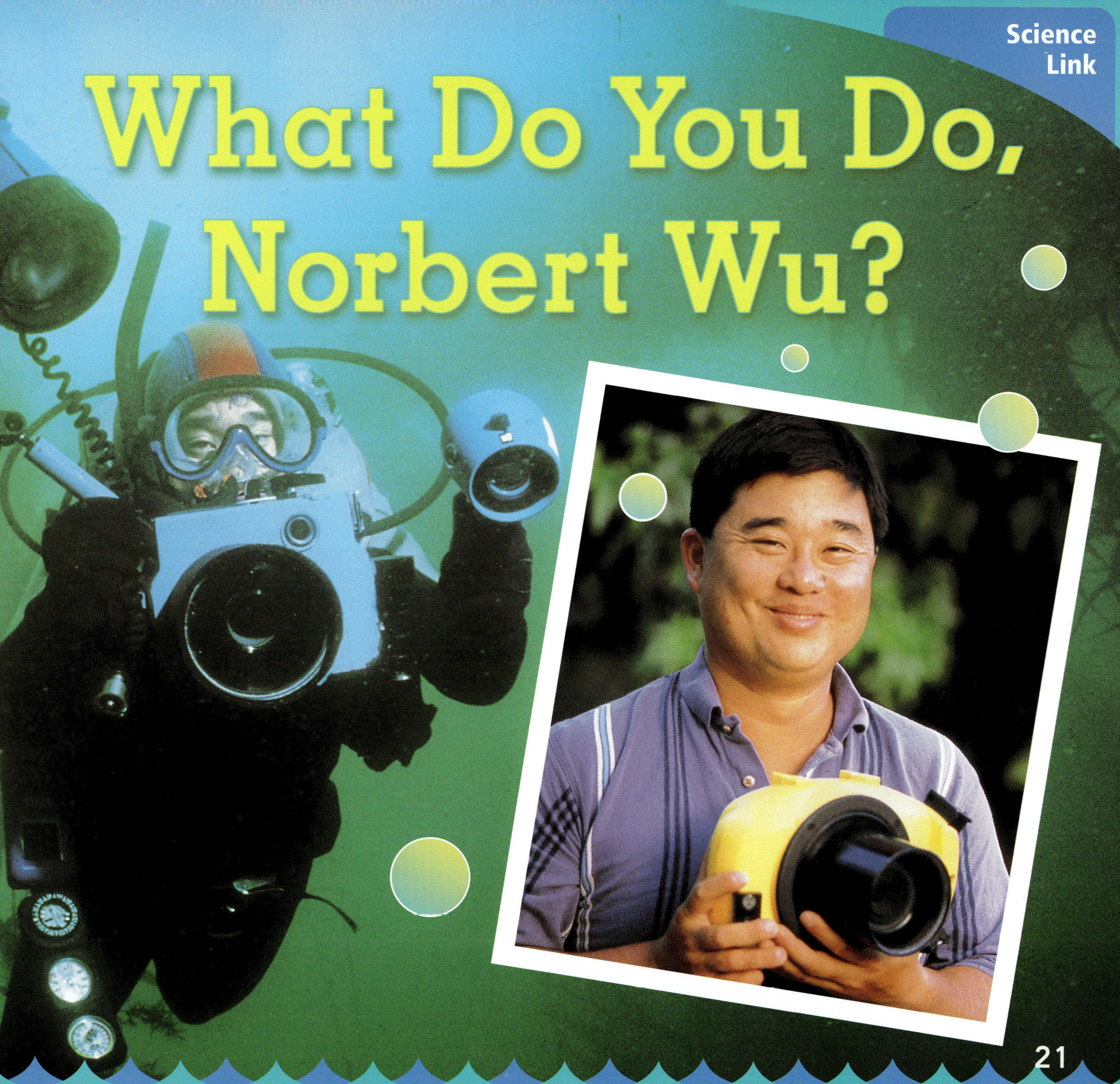

I am a photographer.
I take pictures.

I see a shark!

Click!

I see a starfish!

Click!

I see seals!

Click!

I took these pictures of fish.
Can you find them in this book?